LIVERPOOL
PAST - PRESENT - FUTURE

J. F. SMITH
F.R.S.A., F.S.A. (SCOT.)

GORDON HEMM
A.R.I.B.A.

Alderman A. ERNEST SHENNAN
J.P., M.A., F.R.I.B.A.

PUBLISHED BY
THE NORTHERN PUBLISHING CO. LTD
LIVERPOOL
1948

As a tribute to long and distinguished service and untiring
interest in the corporate life of Liverpool this book is
dedicated to the gracious memory of

THE RIGHT HON. THE EARL OF DERBY,

K.G., P.C., G.C.B., G.C.V.O., T.D.

Honorary Freeman of the City of Liverpool.

1865—1948

A Scale of 240 Yards

OTIA FECIT

All this River to highwater mark on Cheshire shore is in Lancashire and from Fradsom and Warrington Bridges to the Red Stones in Highlake are within the Liberties of this PORT

The Names & Nᵒ of STREETS &c

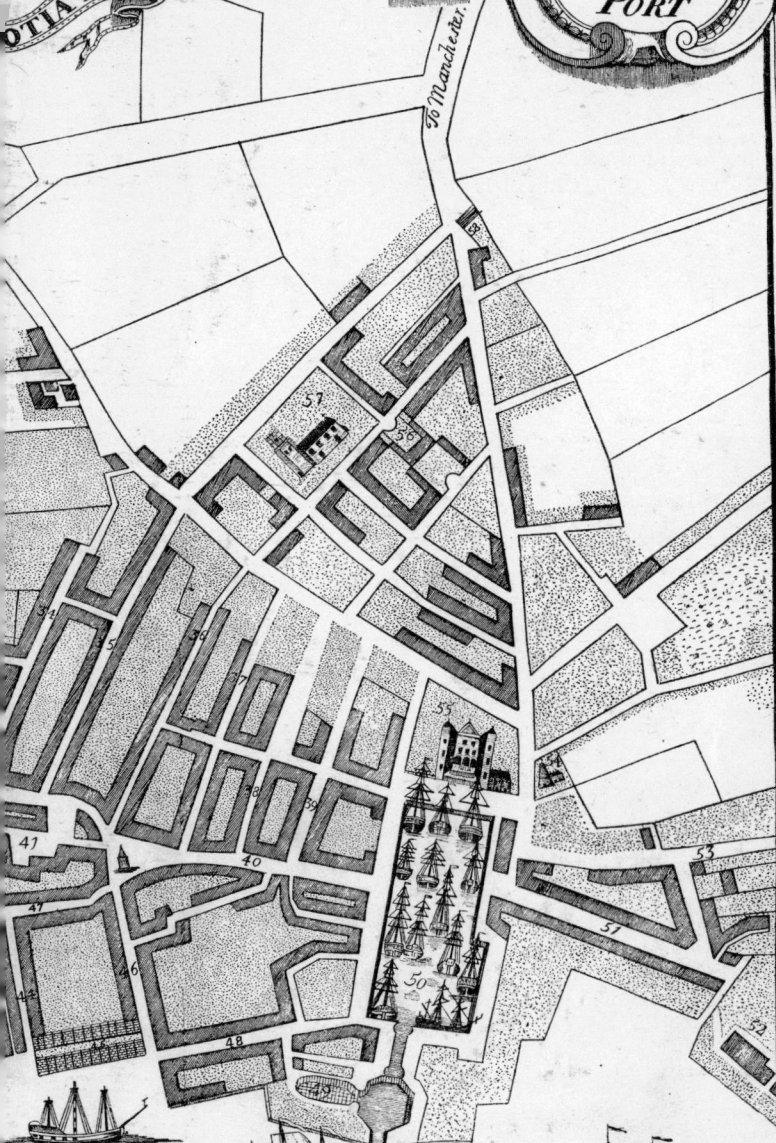

To Manchester

31 Cook Street ....
32 John street ....
33 Sᵗ Thoˢ New buildings .....
34 Harrington street .....
35 Lord street ....
36 Cable street ....
37 Thoˢ street ....
38 Atherton street .....
39 King street ....
40 Pool Lane ....
41 New Market ....
42 Castle Hill ....
43 Moor street ....
44 James street ....
45 Sea brow ....
46 Redcross str ....
47 Preesons Row ....
48 Strand street ....
49 Dry Dock ....
50 Wett Dock ....
51 Morsey street ....
52 Salt Work ....
53 Park lane ....
54 Glass house y ....
55 Custom house &c ....
56 Charity School ....
57 Sᵗ Peters Churchy .....
58 Alms houses ....
59 Old Alms houses ....
60 Sᵗ Patricks hill ....

M E R S E Y

: tell the

aces ; that

he will be

PSALM 48.

The Water Front, Liverpool — by Gordon Hemm

THE MERSEY.

"At all seasons, at all states, the River was beautiful. At dead low water, when great sandbanks were laid bare, to draw multitudes of gulls; in calm, when the ships stood still above their shadows; in storm, when the ferries beat by, shipping sprays, and at full flood, when shipping put out and came in, the River was a wonder to me. Sometimes, as I sat aloft in the cross-trees, in those early days, I thought how marvellous it was, to have this ever-changing miracle about me, with mountains, smoky, glittering cities, the clang of hammers, the roar of hoot of sirens; the miles of docks, the ships and attendant ships, all there for me, seemingly only noticed by me; everybody else seemed to be used to it by this time, or to have other things to do."

John Masefield.
— "New Chums" published by Heinemann in 1944.

FOREWORD

Mr. Hemm and those who have joined him in producing this book have rendered a service to the public of Liverpool.

Time marches on; present problems and difficulties occupy our time and not infrequently depress our minds. We need inspiration, and many may find it in the history of Liverpool. It is a city that has been singularly blessed in the past: it has many buildings of beauty: it has succeeded in attracting, and retaining, many businesses of international fame. As a port it is probably one of the best-known places in the world, and the present devastation in the city was Hitler's tribute to the principal port on the western approaches to Britain.

Liverpool will rise again in beauty: it will retain its commercial life, and I hope that industries of greater importance and of a wider range will develop within its municipal boundaries, thereby providing stability of employment for its people.

Meanwhile this small book provides both a guide to the past and present and encourages a stimulating vision of the future of a city worthy of its high tradition.

Woolton

INTRODUCTION

My love of Liverpool goes back to the days when, as an architectural student in that City, I began to discover a wealth of interest in the outward aspect of a vast and rapidly expanding municipality.

I soon found that it possessed a distinctive atmosphere, and that its inhabitants were a kindly and lovable people. I found an inherent beauty in the classical buildings of the 18th and 19th centuries, and in a great modern Cathedral ; a beauty in the ships on a spacious river, and in their dockland setting, a beauty in the stateliness of the surrounding parklands.

At that period life was less strenuous than it is to-day, and the economic situation far less tense. Time passes on, for it is over a quarter of a century since I first set foot in Liverpool, and during the intervening years, events of unparalleled consequences have taken place. Two world wars within a comparatively short period must naturally result in serious repercussions, and to-day the City exhibits anomalies which a decade back would have been counted as incredible.

Liverpool at the present time is in a state of transition, one might rightly say in the melting pot, regarding its future shaping. Many good ideas have been put forward, incorporating aesthetic and practical schemes to make this City truly beautiful.

I have often thought of the significance of Liverpool as a port and City of world wide pre-eminence, with a proud historical past, and the promise of a still prouder future. Like so many other cities and towns suffering from the aftermath of war, it courageously shows a brave face, and although many familiar parts have vanished, the major portion of the townscape still remains for people to realise that on the shores of the Mersey there stands a vital centre, foremost in shipping, commerce and industry.

The need for some informative literature, adequately illustrated, dealing with the past, present and future aspects of Liverpool in one presentable volume is keenly felt. I hope a work of this nature will not only be of value educationally, but will also enliven citizens and visitors to a great appreciation of this fine City.

It is a privilege to incorporate in this book the name of the Right Honourable Lord Woolton, P.C., C.H., D.L., LL.D., who so willingly acceded to my request to write a foreword. For this distinguished patronage I am most grateful.

I am fortunate to have as collaborators Alderman A. Ernest Shennan, J.P., M.A., F.R.I.B.A., and Mr. J. F. Smith, F.R.S.A., F.S.A. (Scot.) the City Librarian. Alderman Shennan, I need hardly say, is an acknowledged authority on architecture and town planning, and as Chairman of the Liverpool Post-War Re-development Committee is extremely well versed to write upon its future.

The realisation of this volume is mainly due to Alderman Shennan, whose close personal interest, wise counsel, and enthusiastic support, has done so much to make this publication possible. For this invaluable help I express my warmest gratitude.

Mr. J. F. Smith, who has made a special study of the City's local history, deals with the past from the days when this great Port was little more than a fishing village. This historical essay, I am sure, will appeal to many who may be acquainted with the Liverpool of to-day, yet possess slight knowledge of its aspects in ancient times. I am indebted to the writer for this excellent retrospective survey.

My thanks are due to the Corporation of Liverpool for so liberally subscribing to this book, to the City Engineer, Mr. Henry T. Hough, M.I.C.E., M.T.P., and his Deputy Planning Officer, Mr. J. J. Davies, M.T.P.I., for many courteous interviews, and for permission to use selected plans and blocks, to the Public Libraries Committee for the right to reproduce from its fine historical collection of water colours, prints and old maps.

I express my gratitude to Sir Lancelot Keay, K.B.E., for the loan of photographs, to Sir Bertram Chrimes, C.B.E., for the two Herdman reproductions, to the Very Rev. Canon J. A. Turner, for the subjects depicting the Metropolitan Cathedral, and to Elsam, Mann & Cooper Ltd. and Stewart Bale Ltd. for many impeccable photographs.

Mr. Charles D. Alexander has ably assisted in the revision of proofs. The Palatine Engraving Co. made most of the blocks, and The Northern Publishing Co., Ltd. has been most helpful throughout the compilation of this book, and for this valuable co-operation I make due acknowledgement.

THE PAST

By J. F. SMITH, f.r.s.a., f.s.a. (scot.)

THE ANTIQUITY OF LIVERPOOL goes back to Saxon times, although there is nothing now existing of its most ancient buildings: the Chapel of St. Mary of the Quay, the Tower and the Castle. At the top of what is now Lord Street, there stood a stone castle, built by William de Ferrers, Earl of Derby, soon after 1235. The Castle was demolished in 1725 and the site used for a market and then a church (St. George's), and later for the present Queen Victoria Monument. Apart from the West Derby Courthouse, built in 1662, the only notable building of any antiquity now remaining in Liverpool is the Old Bluecoat School (1717), which is of architectural merit and possesses a typical forecourt of cobble stones.

What served as an Exchange and Town Hall existed as far back as 1429 under the name of St. Mary's Hall. Originally a thatched building, it was slated in 1567. The second Town Hall and Exchange was built in 1673; this was followed by the present building, built in 1754 from designs by John Wood. On the 18th January, 1795, the roof, dome and interior were destroyed by fire; the building was reconstructed with additions as it stands to-day.

The first recorded event of importance in local history took place on the 28th August, 1207, when King John granted the first charter creating " Liverpool " a free borough. Before that date it was merely a fishing village. A second Charter, granted by Henry III in 1229, conferred upon the merchants the privilege of conducting the buying and selling of merchandise without paying government dues; of electing their own mayor, sheriffs and bailiffs; and of conducting their own local courts of justice. The impetus given by these favours to the expansion and prosperity of the town caused a thorough reorganization of the local industries—agriculture, salt mining and fishing; but a period of stagnation followed, due, possibly, to the unrest caused by the Wars of the Roses, and it was not until the latter part of Queen Elizabeth's reign, with the opening up of the New World, that Liverpool's fortunes and status improved, her geographical position finally establishing her as the premier port to the American continent.

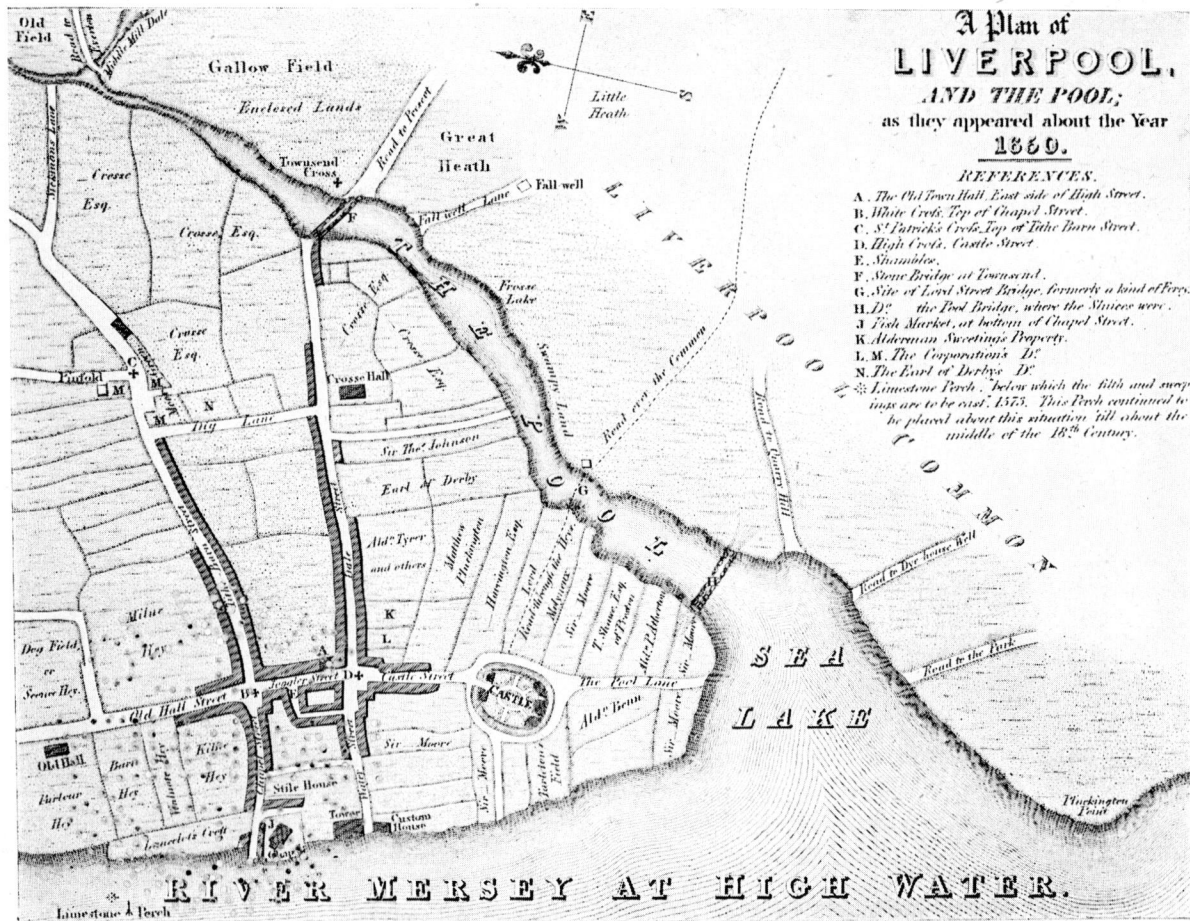

A Plan of
LIVERPOOL,
AND THE POOL;
as they appeared about the Year
1650.
REFERENCES.

A. The Old Town Hall, East side of High Street.
B. White Cross, Top of Chapel Street.
C. St. Patrick's Cross, Top of Tithe Barn Street.
D. High Cross, Castle Street.
E. Shambles.
F. Stone Bridge at Townsend.
G. Site of Lord Street Bridge, formerly a kind of Ferry.
H. Do. the Pool Bridge, where the Sluices were.
J. Fish Market, at bottom of Chapel Street.
K. Alderman Sweeting's Property.
L.M. The Corporation's Do.
N. The Earl of Derby's Do.
* Limestone Perch, below which the filth and sweepings are to be cast. 1575. This Perch continued to be placed about this situation till about the middle of the 18th Century.

Plan of Liverpool in 1650

In the reign of Charles I the town paid £15 ship money with much grumbling and refused to pay any more. The inhabitants further showed their independent spirit by embracing the Parliamentary side in the Civil War, which led to the most outstanding event in the town's history, when in 1644 Prince Rupert carried it by assault. The losses of the inhabitants on that occasion were very great, and though some relief was granted by the Government, most of it fell on the town. Great interest will be found in the study of " The Plan of Liverpool, with the Castle and fortifications as they appeared at the time of the siege in 1644,"* prepared by Sir Bernard de Gomme, officer of engineers to Prince Rupert.

* Copy in Liverpool Public Library.

The plan shews the line of the demolished Roundhead entrenchments, as well as the later fortifications of the Royalist soldiery. The town was retaken by Sir John Meldrum the following November.

The development of the town as a major port is said to have followed the terrible years of the Great Plague in London (1664) and the great Fire there (1666) when many London merchants moved to Liverpool and started business, especially with the plantations, a trade which was very profitable, but which gave rise to the iniquitous slave trade. The normal voyage of a ship engaged in this trade was a triangular one, as follows : the ship sailed from Liverpool laden with goods suitable for barter with native chiefs on the West Coast of Africa in exchange for slaves and, having obtained its human cargo, sailed to the plantations, Jamaica, Demerara or America, where the slaves were sold in the established slave markets. With the proceeds from the sale of the slaves, a return cargo was purchased, consisting of sugar, rum, cotton or tobacco, with which the ship sailed back to Liverpool.

The long continental wars gave rise to privateering, in which Liverpool ships played a great part, and brought into prominence such men as

View of Liverpool from the River Mersey in 1650

Tower of Liverpool at the foot of Water Street in 1680.   View from
the river showing also St. Nicholas' old church

from a water colour by J. McGahey

Fortunatus Wright and William Hutchinson ; the latter wrote a book on
practical seamanship, invented mirrors for lighthouses, and for thirty-five
years continued a series of observations on the tides, the weather and the
winds, which served as data for Holden's Tide-tables.

To give an idea of the size of the town and its commerce—in 1700,
there were 1,142 houses, with a population of 5,714, and the number of
vessels using the port was 80, with a total tonnage of 5,200.   Chadwick's
" Mapp of all the streets, lanes and alleys within the town of Liverpool in
1725 " shews the town with one wet dock (now Canning Place) and one
dry dock (now the Canning Dock), and the suburbs beginning at Old Hall
Street on the north side, at Lime Street on the east, and at Hanover Street

on the south.   It is easy from this map to trace the subsequent spreading of the city over the 27,321 acres it covers to-day and the gradual extension of miles of docks.

The making of the docks had naturally much furthered the use of the port : the Old Dock, built on the site of the Pool and formally opened in 1715, was the second wet dock in England.   Salthouse Dock followed in 1753, George's Dock in 1771 (the noble range of warehouses on the east quay—the Goree Piazzas—were not built until 1793, and, being destroyed by fire in 1802, they were rebuilt in 1806) ; King's Dock was opened in 1788, and Queen's Dock in 1796.   Situate in Canning Place on the east side of the Old Dock was the old Custom House (site now covered by the Sailors' Home).   With the construction of the various docks to meet the increasing trade of the Port, the old Custom House became too small and

West Derby Courthouse built in 1662

from a water colour by Grainger Smith

The Old Exchange (second Town Hall) *c.* 1750 showing the adjoining shops in Castle Street. This structure was taken down in 1755   *from a lithograph by J. McGahey*

inconvenient for the amount of business transacted there. The filling up of the Old Dock being contemplated, the space it occupied suggested an eligible site for a new Custom House, to include also the Excise and a Post Office. This was completed in 1839 from the designs of John Foster and was ultimately totally destroyed by enemy action in 1941.

From the time of the first dock the printed annals of the town record many vicissitudes of fortune, including pestilence, trade stagnation, storms, slave trading and privateering, the influx of poor immigrants from Ireland, great fires and explosions. Notwithstanding all these she held her own in commercial rivalry and was able to undertake great pioneer work in shipping, railways, and canals, the manufacture of pottery and porcelain, watches and clocks.

Canals played a great part in opening up communications between Liverpool and the interior of the country towards the latter part of the eighteenth century. Some of the early canals were constructed by utilizing the tributaries of the Mersey, later the Rivers Mersey and Humber were connected, the Grand Junction Canal was constructed between Liverpool and the pottery and iron districts of Staffordshire, and the Leeds and Liverpool Canal was linked up to the large manufacturing towns in East Lancashire and the West Riding of Yorkshire.

Transport within the borough up to the early 19th century was by sedan-chair and waggon; to distant parts by stage coaches from the inns and taverns in Castle Street, Water Street and Dale Street; and the Mersey was crossed by ferry sail boats plying for hire from the wall slips or stairs. Sailors frequented the many taverns in Paradise Street and Frog Lane (now Whitechapel); the merchants favoured the Coffee houses near the river front, while the intellectuals met in town at the Athenaeum, the Lyceum, the Fireside Club, the Ugly Club, the YZ Club, etc.

The first Liverpool printed book appeared in 1712; the printed newspaper was first issued in 1712, and the first name directory in 1766.

St. Peter's Church viewed from School Lane

from a water colour by S. Herdman
(in the possession of Sir Bertram Chrimes)

View from the bottom of James Street looking north showing the Goree Piazzas and the East Quay of George's Dock in 1860

from a water colour by J. Barter

For a general survey of the borough at that time one should read Enfield's History of Liverpool, published in 1773.

The first steamship to enter the Mersey was " The Elizabeth " (8 h.p.) in 1815, and the first steamer to cross the Atlantic from Liverpool to New York was " The Royal William " which sailed from the Mersey in the year 1838. The number of vessels using the port in 1830 was 11,214.

The Rainhill locomotive trials of October, 1829, culminating in a victory for " The Rocket," started the triumphant progress of railways and the steam locomotive, the outcome of which was the opening of the Liverpool and Manchester Railway in September, 1830, which was promoted by the principal merchants of the town and brought further prosperity.

Early theatres in Blackberry Lane (now Eberle Street) and the Old Ropery were followed by the opening of a theatre in Drury Lane in 1749; later by the Theatre Royal in Williamson Square in

1772. The Adelphi Theatre in Christian Street was first opened as a circus in 1789. The early nineteenth century saw the establishment of several other theatres, notable amongst which was the Royal Amphitheatre (site of the Royal Court), which first opened, also as a circus, in 1826. Several concert halls flourished: the earliest, the Music Hall in Bold Street, was opened in 1786, and the greatest celebrities of the day appeared on its platform. The Portico Rooms in Newington and the Royal Assembly Rooms in Great George Street were popular rendezvous in the 1840's; but in 1846 Liverpool took a major step in erecting the magnificent Philharmonic Hall. This building, erected from the design of John Cunningham, and opened on August 27th, 1849, was celebrated among the singers of the world for its acoustic properties. It was unfortunately destroyed by fire on July 5th, 1933.

The arms of the town were granted in 1797. The motto " Deus nobis hæc otia fecit ", occurs in the first Eclogue of Virgil, and literally

Hengler's Circus on the site of the Municipal Buildings, Dale Street, 1859   *from a water colour by W. Herdman*

Old Buildings on the north side of Lord Street
between Doran's Lane and Whitechapel, 1798

from a water colour by W. Herdman

translated means " God made these comforts for us ", its usual translation
is " God has given us this peace ".

Up to the passing of the Municipal Reform Act in 1835, Liverpool
was ruled by a self elected council, and it was admitted by the Com-
missioners appointed to enquire into the state of Municipal Corporations
that the affairs of the town had been administered in an unusually
enlightened and public-spirited manner.   A notable example of this is
provided by the docks, which were built and maintained by the Corporation until the passing of the Mersey Docks and Harbour Board Act, in
1857.

Queen Victoria's charter in 1880 constituted Liverpool a city, and in the same year the Bishopric was created. The title of Lord Mayor was bestowed in 1893. The foundation stone of the Cathedral was laid 19th July, 1904.

The remarkable growth and expansion of Liverpool from her early trading years to these days of vast overseas trade is admirably illustrated in the maps, plans and views which appeared from time to time, beginning with the conjectural " Plan of Liverpool and the Pool, 1650 ", and Peters' " View of Liverpool from the Mersey ", of the same date.

Old Custom House and Old Dock in 1774   *engraved by E. Rooker, after P. P. Burdett*

Castle Street in 1799 showing St. George's Church

from a drawing by W. H. Watts

Church Street in the 18th Century showing Georgian façades on the site of Cooper's Stores, and the tower of St. Peter's Church in the background

from a water colour by W. Herdman
(in the possession of Sir Bertram Chrimes)

THE PRESENT

By GORDON HEMM, A.R.I.B.A.

To a stranger visiting a city the first impression will invariably become a lasting impression. Bearing in mind this significant fact the best approach to the City of Liverpool is by water from the Cheshire side of the River Mersey, by taking a ferry boat at Woodside, Birkenhead. From the steamer's upper deck the full extent of the longest line of docks in the world is clearly visible. This impressive scene will convey to the beholder something of the magnitude of the second largest port in the country, with its maritime trade routes covering every part of the globe.

In the centre of this panorama are three conspicuous buildings that dominate the Landing Stage approach. These architectural sentinels form the gateway to the City, and comprise the Liver Building, featuring two weighty towers each supporting a liver bird, the Cunard Building with its restful rectangular outline, and the Dock Board Building crowned with a beautifully proportioned dome of emerald green. This trio of conflicting elements has, with the passing of years, become an integral part of this great river front, and although much criticism has been directed against such architectural disunity, nevertheless Liverpool would hardly be Liverpool without these familiar forms.

Farther to the south the static beauty of the Liverpool Cathedral arrests attention. The great central tower, buttressed by twin transepts, is an inspiring sight. With the completion of the nave and west-end the City will possess a building that will rank amongst the world's ecclesiastical triumphs. Rising from the crest of St. James's Mount, it is the most conspicuous landmark on Merseyside. It would appear to be the work of giants when compared with the insignificant irregular roofs that cluster around its base, and follow the sloping land to meet the still more irregular roofs of the dockland sheds. What contrasts—what inconsistency—and what a spiritual climax !

Having set foot in Liverpool from this watery approach, we find the Landing Stage a place of animation and bustling activity, especially during the peak hours when people are rushing to and from the ferry boats. The continual flow of ingoing and outgoing traffic is a feature of the cross-river service. Farther along to the north is the Princes Stage where the great ocean liners and cross-channel steamers berth. To witness the scene on the day of sailing of one of the mammoth liners is an experience not soon forgotten.

Before proceeding to take a look around the City let us pause for a

An aerial photograph showing the approach to the city from the River Mersey

moment to view the lay-out in the foreground of the Pier Head buildings. This fine *place* forms the terminal of the Liverpool Corporation Transport services, and is a scene of continually moving traffic. From this concourse two main arterial roads, Water Street and James Street, penetrate into the heart of the City. Proceeding along the former, we immediately arrive in the commercial zone, with its massive and lofty office blocks. The Overhead Railway, which crosses Water Street at the rear of the Liver Building, should not be overlooked. This high-level railroad runs the full length of the $11\frac{1}{2}$ miles of docks, which include a graving dock the largest of its kind in Europe, and to obtain the best impression of their size and extent, it is advisable to take a round trip, and see at close range the many activities which characterize this busy port.

The Goree Piazzas, which include two oblong shaped structures, are reputed to be associated with the slave traffic in the days when they formed the quay front to St. George's Dock. After passing under the Overhead Railway we are confronted with these gaunt looking blocks, with their façades of begrimed bricks, and weathered, rusticated arches. Continuing along Water Street the cliff-like fronts of the India Building on one side, and Martin's Bank Building on the other, are very impressive. The combined efforts of the architects, Sir Arnold Thornley and Herbert J. Rowse, produced India Building, said to be the largest office block in the country, whilst the Banking Hall of Martin is a striking instance of how marble can be used as a decorative background to a fine architectural setting. In this splendid example Herbert Rowse has used his versatility to the full.

The building with the velvety black walls located so near to the Bank, is a very important civic structure—the Liverpool Town Hall. To many this highly interesting building may seem disappointing, suffering as it does from the loss of a dignified setting, but if people realized the beauty that lies within these sombre walls, this feeling would change to one of

The Gladstone Dock seen from the air

Towers and Spires of Liverpool

The beauty of the fretted skyline of Oxford and Cambridge
architectural silhouettes. In selecting this study of a Liverpool
significance of the dramatic effects resulting from the grouping
viewing this unique ensemble of soaring landmarks, noble and gr
that pervades the scene, a beauty that has been moulded out o
become commonplace but to the artist it will always remain an a

from a drawing by Gordon Hemm

said to be unique, yet there are other cities that can boast of fine
kyline from William Brown Street, the artist has realised the full
of domes, towers and spires seen against a translucent sky.   In
eful in their outlines, one becomes convinced of an inherent beauty
he City's great heritage of the past.   To many the prospect may
ling inspiration.

The Liverpool Town Hall from Castle Street

from a drawing by Gordon Hemm

joy, for a lovelier group of reception rooms could hardly be imagined. King Edward VII described them as " the finest suite of rooms in England." These gems of classic grace, once seen, can hardly be forgotten, for they reflect an age when culture and an appreciation of art meant so much, not only to the specialist, but to the common people.

The Town Hall, designed by John Wood of Bath in 1754, was originally a much smaller structure, the large ballroom annexe to the north, and the south portico being additions, while the present dome was carried out in the early 19th century. On the ground floor of this annexe the City Council assembles for its monthly meetings. In the year 1795 a disastrous fire destroyed all but the outer walls, and the present reception rooms are the work of James Wyatt, (a former President of the Royal Academy), a reconstruction carried out many years after the original architect's death.

This Civic Building with its pronounced domical crown supporting

Martin's Bank Building and the Liverpool Town Hall

Page Nineteen

The large Ballroom, Liverpool Town Hall

from a drawing by Gordon Hemm

a large terra cotta statue of Minerva, forms the architectural climax to the north of Castle Street, a thoroughfare which, before it was blitzed, extended to the extremity of South Castle Street, and was terminated by a stately, classical pile—the Custom House, whose central mass supported a saucer-like dome. Sir Charles Reilly contends that this was the only street in the world where a domed building closed the vista at each end.

Castle Street must not be passed without referring to two notable façades—The Bank of England and the Westminster Bank, which are located nearly opposite each other. The former erected in 1848, is a classic design of much power and contrasting refinements and is very reminiscent of the best work of its architect Professor C. R. Cockerell, who also completed St. George's Hall, after the early death of Harvey Lonsdale Elmes. Designed by R. Norman Shaw in 1901 the Westminster

Bank incorporates an elevation to Castle Street that is somewhat lighter in handling, with a strong vertical accent, showing the architect's fondness for horizontal bandings in alternate course of brick and marble. The steep, pitched roof with its picturesque dormer windows adds height to the vertical accent.

Proceeding along Dale Street, a thoroughfare following the line of Water Street on the other side of the Town Hall, we observe a continuation of the commercial atmosphere with a predominance of big Assurance Offices, noticeable on both sides of this street. The Liverpool & London and Globe, and the Royal Insurance blocks, respectively, are academic examples of civic architecture. The former, reputed to be one of the

A Dale Street Vista. On the left is the fine façade of the Liverpool & London and Globe Insurance Building

A North John Street vista which includes the massive block of the Mersey Tunnel Ventilating Tower to the left of the picture, North House and the Royal Insurance Buildings on the right

Dale Street looking towards the Municipal Buildings with its conspicuous Clock tower.

purest classic buildings in the country, is another example of the creative ability of its designer Professor Cockerell. The latter is conspicuous for its Renaissance-like tower which is crowned with a golden cupola, and for its groupings of window motifs. Let us study the façade in North John Street, and its adjacent neighbour, North House, the latter representing an interesting instance of a commercial building expressed outwardly by lofty vertical planes of brickwork, suggesting the influence of Netherland architecture.

The fine front proves its architect, A. Ernest Shennan, to be an experimentalist, who realizes the possibilities of brickwork as a successful facing material to street façades.

Victoria Street showing the Liverpool Daily Post and Echo buildings   *from a drawing by Gordon Hemm*
(in the possession of the Liverpool Daily Post and Echo Ltd.)

Facing North House, the windowless elevation of a front that forms
the base to a massive rectangular tower, will arouse curiosity. This
masculine and solid piece of architecture represents one of the series of
ventilating towers which Herbert J. Rowse designed in connection with
the ventilation of the Mersey Tunnel. They form a magnificent contri-
bution to modern building, and being nobly conceived, give an added
beauty to the skyline of Merseyside.

Opposite the Royal Insurance Building at the corner of Dale Street, stands the Angel Hotel, an ancient hostelry, the one-time starting point of the London stage-coach. Moorfields is passed on the left of this thoroughfare, and at its climax is the main entrance to Exchange Station. It is but a short walk to the imposing edifice of the former Cotton Exchange in Old Hall Street which, alas, no longer controls the prices of the world's cotton market.

Further along Dale Street, on the right, the pyramidal tower of the Municipal Building catches the eye. This crowning feature to a massive super-structure, blackened by long exposure to the smoke-laden atmosphere, will hardly excite the imagination, especially on a grey day, yet behind these grimy faces there is much good detail exemplifying skilful craftsmanship. Inside this sombre pile are housed the various Municipal Departments, and at all times of the day, busy throngs of people pass along its many spacious corridors.

Remnants of Dale Street as a residential quarter are clearly visible in the smaller properties where some first floor Georgian windows still display their small panes, and the distinctive cornices of that elegant period. Hatton Garden joins Dale Street at the corner of the City Police buildings. The Liverpool Fire Service Headquarters, the Liverpool Corporation Passenger Transport offices, and a Post Office Block are important structures fronting on to this busy cross traffic street.

Directly opposite Hatton Garden is a narrow by-way—Preston Street, which is terminated by Victoria Street. The vista is featured by a prominent "Daily Post and Echo" sign, which is attached to massive building blocks that characterize one side of this spacious thoroughfare. It is here that the famous Liverpool morning and evening papers are printed, while on the opposite side are the lofty premises of the "Evening Express", another well known and widely circulated "Daily." The far end of this street opens out into a prospect of surpassing interest. In the foreground the main entrance to the Mersey Tunnel spreads fan-like, with a dignified marble columnar beacon acting as the pivot, flanked by pavilion-like structures on each side. Sweeping retaining walls are terminated at the rear by a high transverse wall, which acts as a foil to the fine bronze statues of King George V and Queen Mary, the work of the sculptor Sir W. Reid Dick. In the middle distance the elevation of St. George's Hall spreads its classical form the full width of St. John's Gardens. This grand composition, whose source of inspiration is derived from the Greek-Roman styles, is a happy compromise of the massive strength of Roman form with the elegance and grace of Greek detail, and represents

A striking view of St. George's Hall looking from the tunnel approach

one of the few buildings in the world that composes perfectly from whatever angle it is viewed—a proof of great architecture.

Like Sir Giles Gilbert Scott, the creator of Liverpool Cathedral, the architect of St. George's Hall, Harvey Lonsdale Elmes, secured this important undertaking in open competition when still in his early twenties. Although the building is now clothed in a garb of velvety black, its exquisite enrichments, speaking of the noblest period of Greek art, are still discernible. The Corinthian capitals with their superbly carved acanthus leaves crowning the exterior columns and pilasters, add richness and contrast to the large areas of plain walls. The remarkable ingenuity displayed in the plan forms, can only be appreciated by a thorough study of their grouping.

The writer overheard an amusing comment regarding the mistaken identity of St. George's Hall. One of a party of Lancashire sightseers when approaching the vast building exclaimed, " Bygum, theer's Cathedral, ain't it luvly, and wat a bigun "—an observation that seemed to convey to the onlookers one significant quality—that of size.

We must not pass on without some data on the largest sub-aqueous tunnel, which must surely rank as one of the wonders of the world. It links Liverpool with Birkenhead, and through its 2.13 miles of length, a great volume of vehicular traffic passes continually day and night between Lancashire and Cheshire. This tunnel has a width of 36 feet, accommodating four lines of traffic abreast. The total cost of this gigantic scheme was over seven and a half million pounds. July 18th, 1934, was a great

An interesting study of the Queensway tunnel entrance which is dominated by the black marble beacon column

gala day for Merseyside when the late King George V, accompanied by H.M. Queen Mary, performed the opening ceremony.

After passing the Tunnel entrance we feel the steep gradient of William Brown Street. The street alignment on the far side is interesting, containing a series of buildings set well back, whose elevations show traces of strong classic influence. The first from Scotland Road is the Technical College, a comparatively modern structure, and hardly attaining the aesthetic standards of the others in the group. Then follows the Museum, partly blitzed, which embodies an elevation that does not offend the canons of architecture, and gains in effect by the broad flight of steps in front of the portico. Internally there is little left to attract the eye, only a sad reminder of the vandalism of war. The next building in the group is very different in shape and purpose, and outwardly resembles one of the circular Roman temples, and may have been inspired by the Temple of Vesta at Tivoli. It is known as the Picton Library and was designed by Cornelius Sherlock in 1879, and named after Sir James Allanson Picton, a well known historian. A glimpse of the inside reveals a great circular domed hall, which is solely lighted by an eye in the apex of the dome, similar to the Pantheon at Rome. The sweeping curved walls are well lined with books, whose covers of varying shades give colour to the interior. This magnificent library of reference, containing 150,000 volumes, is a Mecca of learning, being much frequented by students and others at all times of the day. It has seating accommodation for over 200 readers in the spacious rotunda. Perhaps the most interesting feature is the collection of old Liverpool drawings and prints, which recall scenes covering many centuries giving fascinating glimpses of the City of yesterday.

Literature and art having much in common, it is not surprising to find the Walker Art Gallery a close neighbour. Its dignified façade is expressive of the home of the arts, with the two flanking statues of Raphael and Michael Angelo commanding the main entrance. This classical exterior is but a blind wall, masking a series of fine picture galleries, which before the building was taken over by the Ministry of Food, housed the City's permanent collection of pictures and sculptures. This collection, which contains many recent acquisitions, is one of the best in the country, and it is to be deplored that these spacious galleries are not available to give the public the opportunity of viewing such artistic treasures.

The Wellington Monument, consisting of a graceful Doric column supporting a figure of the great Duke, forms a pleasant vertical accent set against so much horizontality. A view from the rear of this lofty Monument showing the flanking façade of St. George's Hall, recalls the academic stateliness of a Roman Forum. It is unfortunate that something of this character was not infused into the Station façade facing the Hall. The Victorian Gothic was too powerful an influence for its designer to submit at least to a classic compromise, and consequently the conflict of styles is the lamentable outcome. Unfortunately, the aspiring tendency of the Gothic school resulted in a structure that is entirely out of keeping with the low spreading form of Elmes' building.

The two entrances to the station can hardly be classified as tolerable architecture, least of all the entrance directly from Lime Street. It is hard to believe that a City of the status of Liverpool should suffer from such an

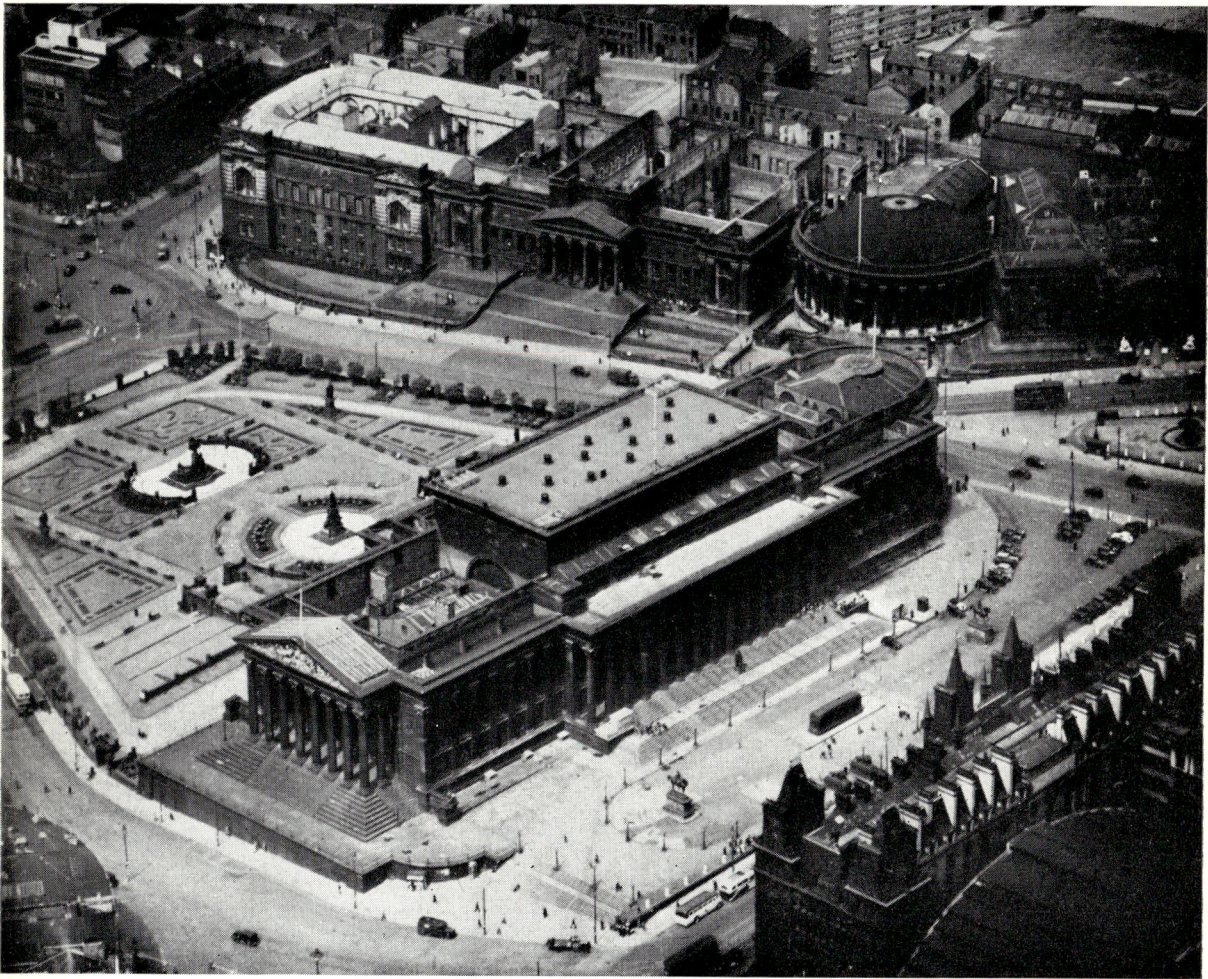

An impressive centre group of buildings which includes St. George's Hall, the Technical College, the Museum and the Picton Library

St. George's Hall from Lime Street

uninspiring approach. What a contrast to that architectural masterpiece opposite ! Let us cross the plateau and view St. George's Hall at close quarters. Take a walk round the building, starting at the impressive south portico, which exhibits a grand sculptural tympanum, with a frieze below containing a Latin inscription which, translated, reads—" Freemen have established a place in Arts, Laws, and Councils." Continuing along the flanking elevation facing Lime Street Station, the huge sixty feet columns supporting a massive lintel (the entablature) must impress many by its monumental grandeur. The same motif is echoed on the east façade, which cleverly breaks away from the rectangular symmetry, by introducing a fine sweeping curve. The spreading elevation to St. John's Gardens, incorporating an upper screen wall with free standing piers supporting an entablature, is indeed civic in scale. It is not surprising to learn that so much praise has been showered upon this exterior by those who are competent to judge.

Internally the same imaginative thought has been expended upon a structure that serves many purposes. Originally, it was planned to accommodate a Hall suitable for secular music, and was the outcome of the enthusiasm of a body of music loving citizens, who, over 100 years ago, subscribed £23,500 for this purpose, because objections were raised to such festivals being held in St. Peter's Church. In the amended scheme prepared by the young architect, the Assize Courts formed an integral part.

A remarkable Hall of Assembly, 151 feet long by 73 feet wide, worthy to rank with those splendid interiors of the Roman Thermae, is the dominating feature of the plan, while the refinement of detail is comparable with the finest qualities found only in the noblest period of Greek Art.

An impression of the great Concert Hall, St. George's Hall, showing the beautiful design of the encaustic tile floor

Shaw's Brow in 1848, now William Brown Street

William Brown Street in 1948

from a drawing by W. Herdman

Photograph by Leonard Card from a drawing by Allan P. Tankard

Rich materials contribute to the sumptuous decorative effect, which includes polished red granite columns, marble and alabaster balustrades, and richly designed gates in bronze. We must not forget the encaustic tile floor which reflects something of the great curved vault in its architectural finesse. The many statues of famous Liverpool citizens placed in niches could hardly have a more appropriate setting. This grand concept was opened to the public in 1854.

The Law Courts planned at each end of the Great Hall have direct access to the latter, while a wide corridor circulating round the place of assembly, communicates with many accessory rooms. A spacious semi-circular entrance at the north end is very well planned and leads into the beautiful small concert room—a gracious interior with a pervading air of Greek refinement noticeable in the elegant enrichments which are modelled almost to perfection.

The Great Hall contains galleries on the first floor, which are entered from a circulating corridor, repeating the similar arrangement on the lower floor. This scholarly interior was damaged through fire and water during one of the Liverpool blitzes in 1941. Unfortunately, the beautiful organ was put out of action. We are thankful that this great fabric was spared from severe damage during the dark days of the war, for in St. George's Hall the City possesses a building that is comparable with that of Liverpool Cathedral, in expressing the highest attributes of art, each in its own respective style.

On St. George's plateau are some important monuments. In the centre is the Cenotaph, designed by Professor L. B. Budden, proportioned so that it does not compete with the scale of a magnificent architectural foil, likewise the flanking crouching lions, grouped in pairs. The equestrian statues of Queen Victoria and Prince Albert, and the pedestal statue of Lord Beaconsfield, are likewise subservient in size, and in no way do they compete in scale with those larger parts.

Lime Street, consisting of small shops, a theatre, cinemas, and hotels, is a busy thoroughfare, much frequented by a cosmopolitan crowd. At its termination stands the Adelphi Hotel, a striking design for this class of building. It was specially built for the American tourist traffic, when Liverpool berthed the " Ocean Greyhounds " of the North Atlantic service. On the opposite side, on a sweeping curved site, is the semi-dismantled Lewis's store. Before it was blitzed it served a very practical purpose, each floor embodying perfect functional planning to accommodate the multitude of shoppers who always counted upon Lewis's as a port of call.

The closing of the vista of Renshaw Street by the tower of St. Luke's Church (a fabric of historical account) is very effective, while above the roofs of the shops the dramatic mass of the Cathedral Tower can be seen when viewed from the lower end of this street. Brownlow Hill with its approach fringing one side of the Adelphi Hotel, leads to the main building of the Liverpool University, after a stiff climb of some ten minutes walking. This important centre of learning represents one of the new Universities, for it was not until 1903 that its Royal Charter was granted. Since that time many of its faculties have achieved greatness, and to-day it enjoys the reputation of being one of the most progressive Universities in the country.

An impression of the rear grouping of the Metropolitan Cathedral taken from a recent model

View of Crypt, Metropolitan Cathedral, the first portion to be completed

Perspective showing the principal front of the
Metropolitan Cathedral, with the great dome
dominating the composition

from a water colour by Cyril A. Farey

Page Thirty-seven

Unfortunately, its architecture hardly befits such high academic standards, for the main building represents a style known erroneously as " cast iron " Gothic. This term may be attributed to the appearance of the pressed brick and terra cotta dressings, which suggest a soulless rigidity reminiscent of cast iron work. The responsible architect, Alfred Waterhouse, was a strong adherent of the Gothic revival school which is clearly reflected in this design.

The Cohen Library, a close neighbour in Ashton Street, forms one of the latest additions to the University, and is a fine example of how a building of this character should be planned, and how it should appear externally. It is the work of Mr. H. A. Dodd, a former student of the Liverpool School of Architecture.

The Metropolitan Cathedral, located nearly opposite the University, was designed by the late Sir Edwin Lutyens, and will eventually be crowned by a great dome 168 feet in diameter. The series of barrel vaults which characterize the great interior are in direct contrast to the sweeping pointed arches of the Anglican Cathedral. A study of the plan, sections, and elevations shows the remarkable creative mind of the designer, stamped by great powers of originality.

"Stupendous", one will surely exclaim, when it is realized that the central archway to the West Front will rise to the height of the University tower. Although it may take over one hundred years to complete this vast building, one day a magnificent silver dome will rise heavenwards above the medley of the City's rooftops. What could be more inspiring to ocean travellers upon entering the Mersey than to witness the silhouette of Liverpool crowned by the world's two most beautiful religious landmarks of modern time—a superb dome and a superb tower.

The crypt is nearing completion. The first section consisting of three chapels, is finished. In one of the chapels lies the first Archbishop of Liverpool, Dr. Whiteside, and at its entrance is the remarkable Rolling Gate. The long crypt corridor has been in use for some time, and is a very impressive interior 265 feet long by 28 feet wide.

At the lower end of Ranelagh Street, under the shadow of Lewis's, is Central Station, the smallest of the three railway termini. It can at least boast of a front of some architectural respectability. The congested approach to the station will eventually be freed, when the inner ring road is constructed, and the present alignment of uninspiring shop fronts will be replaced by something more uniform in design and something more worthy of a station place.

Bold Street, Hanover Street, and Church Street, are close on the heels of Central Station. Bold Street, once the aristocratic rendezvous of wealthy Liverpolitans, has now changed in character, due mainly to the ravages of war, and many of the former elite shopping establishments are now occupied by some of the middle-class city stores. St. Luke's Church tower closes the vista of yet another street, and looking to the top of Bold Street we view this arresting climax. From Bold Street, it is but a short walk to Rodney Street, the preserve of the medical profession and which, in former days, was a fashionable residential quarter, as the many elegant Georgian fronts indicate. The dignified classic house where W. E. Gladstone, the great Victorian Prime Minister was born, can be located by a plate inserted in the wall, recording this historical event. It has a fine entrance doorway, and windows that express a sincerity of purpose, a conspicuous attempt to produce good design out of good proportioning.

The shopping centre of the City, Church Street

Rodney Street showing the house with the pediment where W. E. Gladstone was born

Talking of the medical profession brings to mind another building that must not be overlooked—the Medical Institution. This moderately sized structure stands near the top of Brownlow Hill, and despite its blackened exterior, its distinctive design, containing the Ionic order, is rarely overlooked. Its architect, Clark Rampling, saw his task accomplished in 1837. The building serves the purpose of a headquarters and library for the medical profession. The plan includes a lecture theatre and a small Council Chamber. As one of the smaller contributions to the best classic buildings of Liverpool, it holds a high place.

At the southern end of Rodney Street we behold the tremendous mass of the Cathedral filling the skyline. It is a pity we cannot view the exterior in its finished state, for the absence of the Nave and West End (yet to be built) produces a feeling of unbalance due to the massive temporary wall enclosing the main arch to the Central Space.

There is so much beauty and interest to be found both inside and outside this ecclesiastical masterpiece that to do full justice to the building would require a very stout volume. For the interest of readers the following dimensions will give some idea of the titanic size of Sir Giles Scott's remarkable design.

The total length of the building is 619 feet, and with the exception of St. Peter's, Rome, this is unrivalled by any other Cathedral. The great vault covering the Central Space rises to 176 feet, being the highest vault in the world, while the Vestey Tower is 331 feet measured from the sanctuary floor to the crowning parapet walls. The width across Transepts is 197 feet and the width across Choir and Choir Aisles is 87 feet.

Liverpool Cathedral from the air

from a drawing by Gordon Hemm

Liverpool Cathedral from St. James's Road   *from a drawing by Gordon Hemm*
(in the possession of Sir Bertram Chrimes)

The Central Space, Liverpool Cathedral   *from a drawing by Gordon Hemm*

Auditorium, Philharmonic Hall

The fabric was commenced in 1904, and the first section of the building was consecrated 20 years later in the presence of King George V and Queen Mary. The Lady Chapel was completed in 1910. Since the work started, building operations have never ceased, although progress was slowed up during the two World Wars. It is expected that another 20 years will elapse before this great undertaking will be completed.

Not far from Rodney Street is the Philharmonic Hall, a conception that is rather Germanic in design outwardly, yet inwardly embodying a beautiful Hall of Music, perfect both architecturally and acoustically. Its architect, Herbert J. Rowse, has produced a building worthy of the old " Phil.", ideally suited for its purpose, imposing in mass, and delicate in detail. Sir Malcolm Sargent must have felt inspired when conducting his famous orchestra in an interior that almost resounds with another kind of music.

Before passing into Duke Street it is interesting to observe the architecture around Hope Street, Gambier Terrace, along Upper Parliament Street, and on to Falkner and Abercromby Squares. Amidst all this array of Georgian charm, one momentarily feels transformed to another age—an age when architects welded those small domestic units into long terraced façades, on a scale that almost vies with the architecture of the grand manner.

Off Hope Street adjacent to the School of Art in Mount Street, is the bold front of the Liverpool Institute. It was formerly known as the Mechanics' Institution, and since 1825, the year it was opened, many additions have been made to the original structure. According to Picton, it was not a success as an evening school for the study of mathematics, chemistry, and the art of design. Eventually it was established as a day school, offering the best education at the lowest fees. Its designation was

Abercromby Square from Bedford Street

The Assembly Hall, Liverpool Institute   *from a drawing by Allan P. Tankard*

then changed to the Liverpool Institute. The architect entrusted with this educational project, A. H. Holme, was a disciple of the Greek Revival movement, an influence strongly mirrored in the external and internal features of this solid academic design.

Some of the old house fronts in Duke Street are worthy of inspection. This thoroughfare runs from the climax of Rodney Street right into the heart of the City. Half-way down is Colquitt Street, a street that will always be known, if only for one famous building, The Royal Institution. This elegant structure was erected in 1799 as a private residence, and at that time it was the ideal exemplification of a town house, planned on a most liberal scale. Internally it possessed an atmosphere of cultural grace, with many finely proportioned rooms, large enough to do justice to the cumbersome crinoline dresses of the Georgian ladies. Its life as a private home was short, for in 1817 it became the Home of the Royal Institution founded by Henry Roscoe for the promotion of literary, artistic, and philosophical societies. Externally the building reflects something of this cultural significance, especially in its main front, pleasant balanced grouping, orderly distribution of windows, an entrance that bespeaks a pristine classic beauty, and distinguishing qualities found only in the best Georgian architecture.

Colquitt Street meets Bold Street at its far end, and proceeding down the latter we notice on the right the dark doors of the Lyceum Club, a building showing classic influence. The main frontage faces Bold Street, and comprises a recessed portico containing six graceful Ionic columns. The two flanking walls each contain a window with attached column surrounds, framed by a suppressed segmental arch, and form pleasing elements in a design containing more wall space than windows.

The Lyceum, Bold Street

Internally are rooms of interesting shapes, the most pleasing being the Rotunda, a spacious circular hall as the name implies. This interior housed the Liverpool Library which was founded in 1758 and ranked as the oldest lending library in Europe. As this building was opened in 1801, it is not surprising to find Greek influence in evidence in much of the detail. The dome of the Rotunda exhibits a delightful continuity of delicate patterns applied chiefly to the concave ribbed surfaces between the panels. The balcony encircling the walls at first floor level has no visible supports, and is cantilevered from the wall.

The News Room, of liberal size, originally possessed a fine scale, before the curved ceiling was dismantled to make way for a flat one at a lower level. The wind barometer, resembling the shape of a clock, which occupies a central position in the wide recess, is well worthy of notice as it is one of the few specimens extant in Europe. The bas-relief panels, long and narrow, contain figure compositions that are very Grecian in feeling, and the same influence is clearly discernible in the profiling of the details in this room. The three sculptured panels to the elevation facing Church Street, represent Art, Science, and Geography, and here there is the same classic influence.

Opposite the Lyceum's main front, the Liverpool Gas Company's façade towers above all adjacent structures. It is a design modern in feeling yet respecting tradition, and does not quarrel with the neighbouring Georgian and Victorian fronts. The architects, Quiggin and Gee, concentrated their ingenuity on the internal aspect of this impressive structure. The skilful application of different kinds of marbles to form artistic backgrounds to enhance the display of this Company's products, is a striking instance of the value of this material. Incorporated in the plan is a fine exhibition and lecture room, where many of the leading expositions relevant to the City's trading are housed.

Very impressive is the Cripps shop front with its unusually large areas of plate glass extending to the second floor ; and higher up the street, Bacon's two elevations express much individuality on the part of their designer. It was originally planned as a theatre, yet its outward appearance does not suggest that the building was ever used for dramatic performances.

Upon entering Church Street, one is confronted with important shopping stores, which align both sides of this popular thoroughfare—Boots, Burtons, Woolworths, C. & A. Modes and Coopers dominate one side, while the Bon Marché, Marks & Spencers, Hendersons, and Bunneys are conspicuous blocks on the other side. Clayton Square, which communicates with Church Street by means of Parker Street, was once a peaceful residential area, but to-day its character has entirely changed. The frontages of Owen Owen's and Brown's, bear witness to the progressive growth of the City in the rapid development of retail shopping stores, offering every facility for buying in comfort. The Liverpool Market, hardly a stone's throw from this square, occupies the full length of one section of Great Charlotte Street, and at its extremity on the other side is the Royal Court Theatre, a striking example of a modern building faced with brick, designed by T. Wainwright & Sons. Queen's Square being one of the old squares of Liverpool, it is not surprising to find at its far end a building imbued with the qualities that we associate with good Georgian design—this is the Stork Hotel, which is characterized

Church Street of to-day looking towards Central Station, showing the massive block of Coopers Store on the right

Williamson Square

from a drawing by Grainger-Smith

by a frontage of academic proportions. This square has witnessed many changes from the days when it possessed a residential air, to the present time, when on every morning of the week the enclosed space is strewn with the products of market gardeners and attendant traffic vehicles of all kinds. We try to picture the same square as it appeared one hundred years ago, a quiet retreat laid out with green trees. Crinolines and top hats gave the finishing touches to a delightful Victorian setting.

Not far from Queen's Square is Williamson Square, another place of antiquity, which includes the Old Theatre Royal erected in 1772, now used as a cold storage depot. It was one of the Patent theatres and many famous Victorian artistes walked its boards, including Sir Henry Irving.

The Playhouse, formerly the Star Music Hall, prominently placed on a corner site, carries on the traditions of the English drama. It has produced many stars of stage and screen fame. From this square we pass into Basnett Street, a narrow shopping thoroughfare, yet containing such well known stores as George Henry Lee's and the Bon Marché, part of the latter fronting on to Church street.

Amid this pervading modern atmosphere, hardly a stone's throw from Church Street, and standing in a secluded backwater, is the Old Bluecoat Hospital, now called Bluecoat Chambers, which to-day exhibits the scars of war, much of the upper floor having disappeared. Fortunately the surrounding walls remain, thus retaining something of the old world character of this delightful central block and projecting side wings. Built in 1777, it is a scholarly example of the early Georgian style with elevations of brick and stone dressings, that express charm and dignity. This famous charitable school was founded by Bryan Blundell, and was erected out of money collected from various sources, and since its opening it has been the means of rescuing poor children from dire poverty, feeding and educating them, and sending them out into the world with the prospects of secure and prosperous careers. It is hoped that a genuine restoration of the damaged fabric will one day be accomplished, for such genuine examples of period architecture are rare in this City, and are of the utmost value from an architectural standpoint.

The old Bluecoat Hospital, now Bluecoat Chambers

from a drawing by Geoffrey Wedgewood

The uncoordinated façades of Lord Street with Church Street viewed in the distance

Before leaving Church Street to enter Lord Street, we must not overlook a narrow and lofty structure which formerly was a branch of Martin's Bank. It is located directly opposite C. & A. Modes and is another instance of the aesthetic possibilities of the use of brickwork as a facing material. In design it strikes a new note, and one feels that its architect, Herbert J. Rowse, must have derived much pleasure in creating those two charming little façades which reflect something of the innate spirit of the northern Italian Romanesque style.

To-day Lord Street appears vastly different from the Lord Street of pre-war days. The southern side, except for one gaunt looking shopping block, is one vast open space. We have to thank Hitler for this amenity, though it would appear to be poor compensation for all the tragedy of bombing. The calamity of war has been the means of giving breathing space to one of the most congested parts of the city, and I hope that a liberal portion will remain as such, perhaps as permanent gardens, in the years that lie ahead.

The top-end of Lord Street intersects with Castle Street, and the devastated South Castle Street. The rather lonely vigil of the Queen Victoria Memorial, located on the site of the old Liverpool Castle, seems to have had few admirers, as it is claimed by many to be the ugliest monument in England. Strangely, it has survived intact, while most of the property around was laid flat in those fierce bombing raids of 1941. One cannot say that many of its component parts are ugly, in fact some of the bronze figure groups are extremely well modelled, especially the crowning feature of the dome. It is the band-stand-like conception that upsets our artistic senses, producing the wrong note to a subject of this kind. There

The much criticised Victoria Monument which stands on the site of the old Liverpool Castle

The Goree Piazzas looking towards James Street. The nearer block was badly damaged by enemy action in 1941

from a drawing by Gordon Hemm

is a consequent loss of classic dignity, a quality which is vitally essential to a design of this character.

James Street which leads to our starting point, the Pier Head, is a short thoroughfare of contrasts, with a building here and an open space there, very different from the continuous building frontages, which before the war were its chief features. Towards its lower end, the former White Star Building (badly damaged by bombing) ranks as one of the City's most potential structures of the early twentieth century. It was designed by R. Norman Shaw, the architect of the New Scotland Yard, and its influence is discernible in the elevations of this important Liverpool building.

Before passing the Overhead Railroad, another aspect of the Goree Piazzas is worthy of more than a passing glance, for it represents one of the most romantic spots in the City. The Piazzas were named after the island of Goree, taken from the French in 1759, in commemoration of their associations with the African trade.

Between the high level railroad and the Dock Board building, is the

An arresting study of the exterior of the Mersey Tunnel Ventilation and Control Station

Liverpool's massive commercial buildings seen from the air. In the foreground the three diversely proportioned structures—Liver, Cunard and Dock Board Offices are conspicuously seen

Mersey Tunnel Ventilation and Control Station, which stands on the site of the old George's Dock. It is finely conceived, distinctly modern in feeling, reticent in detail, and ranks among the best architectural contributions to Merseyside. As we approach the Pier Head, a close-up view of the southern façade of the Dock Board building will impress many people by its solidity and strong effects of light and shade due to the weathering of the Portland Stone. This is further revealed in the angle view showing the main frontage in conjunction with this elevation.

A glimpse of St. Nicholas' Church can be obtained from the other end of this spacious traffic place. It is the parish church of Liverpool and ranks as the oldest Anglican fane in the City. The present tower, graceful and lofty, is of 18th century times. The earlier church is shown on the map of 1650 and the tower from the earliest days has formed a conspicuous landmark, so often featured in engravings.

The interior was gutted in 1941 by enemy action and only the outer walls remain. To-day there is a church within a church, a temporary brick fabric covering two-thirds of the ancient nave, an anomaly which is perhaps unique in the annals of English church planning.

Farther afield from the heart of Liverpool are to be found more than one " stately home of England." Speke Hall, recently handed over to the Corporation of Liverpool by the National Trust, is widely known for its beautiful architecture in the picturesque so-called half-timbered

St. Nicholas' Church Tower from the Strand   *from a water colour by Grainger-Smith*

The Entrance façade, Speke Hall

from a drawing by Gordon Hemm

SPEKE HALL

The evolution of English domestic architecture forms a long and fascinating story. During the Tudor era many stately homes were built, and none is more redolent of the vernacular spirit than the beautiful house of Speke.

It has been referred to as a fine example of Elizabethan architecture, although it was commenced in the reign of Henry the Seventh, on the site of an earlier stone structure pulled down in 1490. Unlike its forerunner, the existing building is of timber construction, supports on a stone base, a system of interlacing wood framework that gave unusual opportunities for picturesque grouping to walls and gables.

Quadrangular in plan, its chief feature is the Great Hall, but there are many other apartments that will attract attention, exemplifying superb craftsmanship. A quaint stone bridge, remnants of a moat, and two Yew trees in the Courtyard, are venerable adjuncts to this peaceful and sequestered home of other days.

KNOWSLEY HALL

The most impressive aspects of Knowsley Hall (for centuries the seat of the Earls of Derby) are from the air, which show to the best advantage the fine architectural grouping of the various buildings.

Unlike Speke Hall, with its buildings arranged around a rectangular courtyard, Knowsley resembles the letter L in its general lay-out. The earliest portion of the existing fabric, the south end of the east wing, was built in 1730, and there followed many additions at later dates.

The 18th century work is very graceful, and reminiscent of the high qualities found only in the best Georgian design. Sweeping lawns and well laid out flower beds enhance the architectural setting of this stately hall, which is framed by dense masses of nature's richest greens.

An aerial prospect of Knowsley Hall

The main approach to Croxteth Hall

style, and in this respect it has few rivals in the country. Of early Tudor date it is characterized by a quadrangular layout, moated, and approached by an ancient stone bridge. Internally there is a wealth of interesting antiquities, spacious rooms that exemplify the glory of English craftsman-ship. No other fabric has a greater claim to antiquity within the City boundary, and no other fabric will give greater pleasure to the people who spend an afternoon inspecting the wealth of artistry by the best of Tudor craftsmen.

Knowsley Hall, the seat of the Earl of Derby, and Croxteth Hall, the ancestral home of the Earl of Sefton, are mansions later in date, ex-hibiting Renaissance influence, when the architecture of these great houses followed not the free irregular intricacies of the Gothic style, but the formal regularity of the academic classic phases.

Situated about six miles to the south-east of the centre of the City, and bounded on one side by the estate of Speke Hall is the Liverpool Airport, which occupies a site of 418 acres. Ranking among the finest of its kind in the country, it includes three runways of 1,666 feet, 1,433 feet, and 1,033 feet, surrounded by a broad perimeter track.

An imposing curved building of great length embodies the admini-strative offices and hangars. An imposing central control tower attached to the façade facing the river, dominates the composition, and forms a landmark and guiding beacon for the planes that ply regularly between London, Isle of Man, Belfast, Dublin and Renfrew.

Eventually this great Airport will play its part as a strategic centre in the expansion of the vast network of air routes covering the British Isles and European services.

In summing up the Liverpool of to-day, we first think of great ships, then of vast commercial and industrial activities, and the immensity of the trading estates of Kirkby and Speke. It holds a foremost place in architectural and engineering achievements, in the triumphs of the Cathedral and the Mersey Tunnel. In municipal housing Liverpool has accomplished much, and the residential layouts and fine blocks of flats,

The station buildings at Liverpool Airport, now nearing completion. Dominating the picture is the most up-to-date control tower, and the triple terracing for the general public will be noted

The Old and the New

Page Sixty-two

the product of the creative genius of Sir Lancelot Keay, stand as models which have become the envy of the world.

The University of Liverpool with the brilliant achievements in its School of Tropical Medicine, in scientific research under Sir James Chadwick, and its School of Architecture under Sir Charles Reilly, has established an international reputation, whilst in the realm of the drama the Playhouse has produced many stage and screen stars of outstanding fame.

Well may we be proud of the Liverpool of our generation, just as were the people who lived and laboured here in the past. To the generations yet to come, there is hope, for the wisdom of present day planners is taking the long perspective view, so that the Liverpool of the future will be a place of unrivalled beauty, worthy of the fine traditions of a great Port and a great City.

Speke—the first factory erected by the Corporation

Municipal Housing—St. Andrew's Gardens

THE FUTURE

By Alderman A. ERNEST SHENNAN, M.A., J.P., F.R.I.B.A.

"Out of strength", runs a cryptic Biblical saying, "came forth sweetness". Liverpool is great, and has a future incalculably greater. Can we of this generation evolve for our City the maximum of material and spiritual good, building on the achievements of our predecessors and conjuring phœnix-like a new city out of the enormous evil of the war?

No student of history is likely to delude himself into supposing that what happened to Liverpool during the 19th century could have been avoided under the conditions, national and international, then prevalent. Phenomenally rapid growth overwhelmed a gallant little town which could not, of course, have foreseen the coming of steam navigation, the fuller development of the United States and Empire mass movements of population or the peculiarities of unemployment in a great modern port, such as arose through the Irish famine. Looking back upon the weltering demands of those times, one can but wonder that the town managed as well as it did, advancing steadily in prestige and commercial power while wrestling with domestic social problems towards whose solution it possessed totally inadequate statutory powers. Yet the town's very embarrassments inspired it to a truly remarkable range of reforms as well as philanthropies. "Out of the wreck I rise" was true then as now; and we remember with gratitude great municipal pioneer planners in various spheres, such as William Henry Duncan, James Newlands and George Frederick Deacon.

Nowadays there is at times a tendency, as would-be reformers survey our rich but somewhat chaotic heritage, to disparage our townsmen of the past. That sentiment I cannot share. We had many fine and noble-hearted men and women, battling with bewildering new social problems against heavy odds. Where and why they may have failed is a point profitable to explore; and I venture to suggest that for the success of all municipal planning there are three essentials:—There must be large and bold vision, adequately and courageously carried into practical effect; the city must encourage, not stifle, the enterprise of its citizens, taking them candidly into its confidence when promulgating vast plans for the benefit of all; and we must always remember what perhaps our Victorian fore-fathers sometimes forgot, that beauty of environment, with all the dignity, health and contentment it spells for our citizens, is the only true

View of model showing suggested redevelopment of the Strand and Chapel Street area

Liverpool of the future will spring from the city of to-day, war-torn and depressing as it is. But, unlike the old, the new growth will be authoritatively controlled by a long-term planning policy. That policy began to take form even during the Second World War, and is now sufficiently developed to afford at least a general idea of what will be the shape of local things, say, towards the close of the present century.

Of course, no attempt is being made to settle rigidly and for ever the future of every square yard of land. Our attempt is to determine, by means of a master plan, the broad lines to which future development and re-development shall conform.

NEW SPEED-WAYS.

Governing the whole lay-out must of course, be a basic road system. Good, wide roads are essential to the city and port for internal transport, for inland traffic to and from our docks and warehouses, and for the passage of long-distance through vehicles. Of all such traffic we are bound to cater for an immense multiplication. Arterial roads will radiate, from an Inner Ring Road, towards Preston, Manchester, Warrington and Widnes. These will operate in combination with a series of Ring Roads, extending from an Inner Ring designed to encircle the civic and commercial centre, to the Outer Ring, of which a considerable portion will be outside the present city boundaries.

It is obvious that, if adequate speed is to be achieved with a maximum of safety, these roads, radial and ring, must be as few as possible, and their true purpose must be safeguarded. The practice of fronting buildings on to main roads and of providing parallel service roads will disappear. Considerable ingenuity will, of course, be called for in the designing of the Radial and Ring Road junctions, so as to allow traffic to flow smoothly and safely ; and very heavy cross-traffic may compel the introduction of fly-over crossings.

A MODEL RING ROAD.

As to the Inner Ring Road, its main function will be to divert as much as possible of the traffic converging on the centre of the city, and to cause it to travel *round* rather than *across* the commercial core.

Such a scheme is already essential to relieve congestion ; but without it, in very few years from now, we should have chaos. This road will, it is believed, become a pattern of its kind. It will be provided with wide, dual carriage-ways capable of accommodating a great volume of traffic. The number of its junctions with other highways will be kept to a minimum by the elimination, where possible, of direct entry from minor roads. It will be flanked with ranges of buildings of good architecture, while ample spaces will be reserved for use as promenades, comparable with those of the ring roads of continental cities, the opportunity to provide which was, by the way, afforded by the removal of the medieval town walls.

We have to be practical, and do not intend to destroy our more valuable properties. The Inner Ring Road will follow, as far as practicable, the lines of existing streets, and so will not over-run the principal existing buildings. Following Chapel Street and Tithebarn Street, it will cross Scotland Road in the vicinity of Scotland Place : then, turning southward, will follow Lime Street and Hanover Street to join the line of the

View of model showing suggested redevelopment of the Central Area, showing Ring road

present Dock Road. Thus it will closely connect the three railway termini of Exchange, Lime Street and Central. It will also relieve Lord Street and Church Street of the heavy passing traffic they at present carry, leaving them free to fulfil their proper medium as shopping streets, in an atmosphere of greater elegance and tranquillity.

Financially, this Ring Road is a sound proposition apart from the communal saving of time by traffic efficiency; it will, in the first place, eliminate the necessity for a number of very costly improvements in the city core to accommodate the traffic now to be diverted from it, while in the second place it will greatly enhance site and rateable values along its line of route.

THE ENCLOSED AREAS.

So far, I have considered these main roads only as improved channels of traffic. They will, however, also form boundaries of built-up areas— civic, commercial, industrial, cultural, shopping and residential areas which together make up a city. The new planning as I have suggested will concern itself not only with the traffic problem, but with conditions of life, work and leisure of citizens generally; especially the provision of fresh air, sunshine, the means of culture, entertainment, and recreation; and immunity from all avoidable casualties.

The in-filling of these areas, it can readily be realized, will determine the future make-up of Liverpool. What is to be its nature? Let us first glance at the central area within the Inner Ring Road; this, to be devoted to administration, commerce and the retail trades, requires to be kept free from fast and heavy vehicles, and so it will be. Forty or fifty years hence this area will have been altered beyond all recognition, and according to present proposals will certainly strike a new note in planning and in architecture.

THE FIRST SEGMENT.

Take the devastated section lying between Lord Street and South Castle Street, and the less seriously damaged part to the east of that, extending as far as Lime Street. Re-development here in the comparatively near future will render possible the construction of that section of the Inner Ring Road which will traverse the area from Elliot Street to the bottom of South Castle Street. That will be the first segment of the Inner Circle to be developed, an entirely appropriate beginning; and I am hoping that work upon it will not be much further delayed.

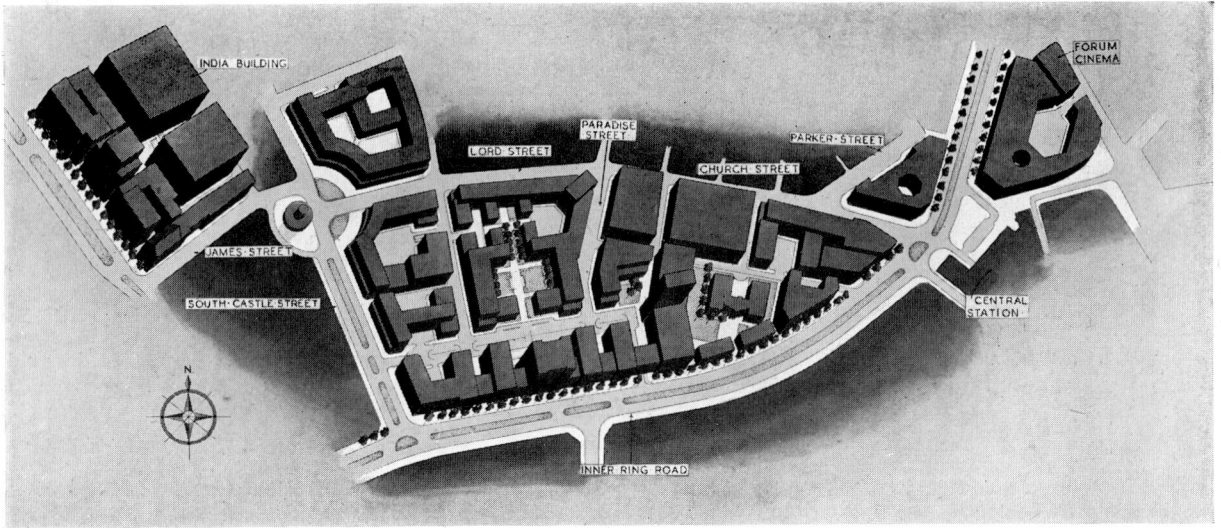

This drawing gives a clear impression of how the first portion of the central shopping and office area of the new Liverpool will look after redevelopment

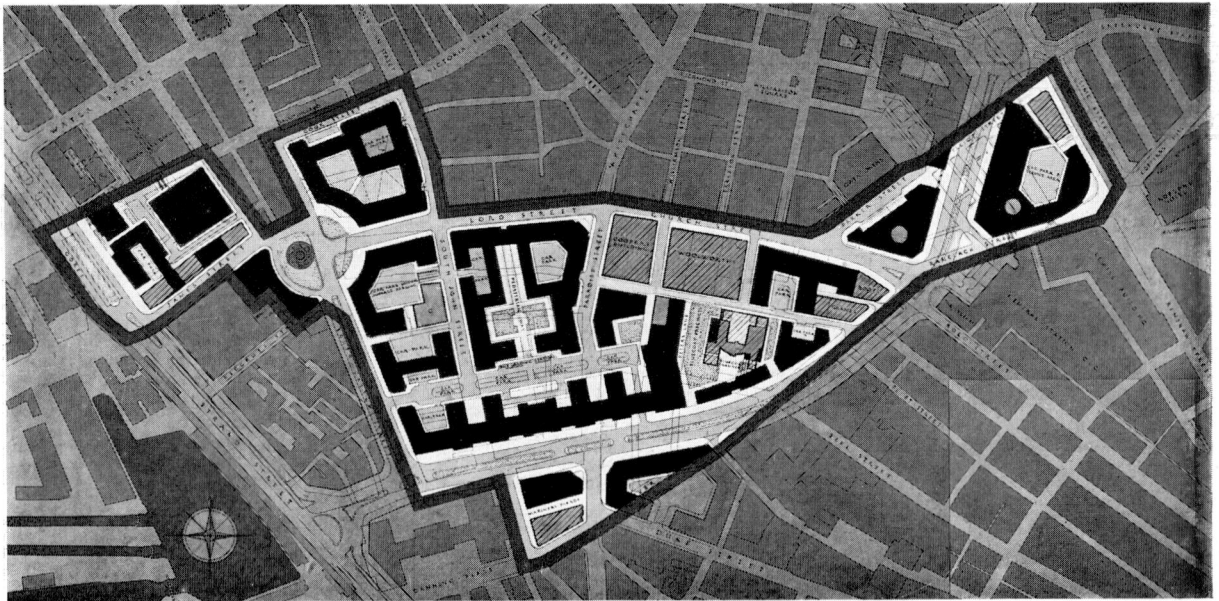

This plan shows the layout relating to the drawing shown above

The existing street pattern there will be considerably altered deliberately in order to limit access to the Inner Ring Road. Paradise Street and South John Street at present connecting respectively with Hanover Street and Canning Place will both, at their southern ends, be closed by large blocks of buildings of a light industrial or warehousing character, to replace those buildings which in pre-war days housed the printing trade. These two roads will, however, be connected by a wide traffic-way, its centre devoted to car-parking. A bus-loading station too may be established there, the spot affording ample accommodation for the loading and unloading of vehicles. Where possible, buildings will enclose their own private car-parks, though there will also be public parking and multi-storey garages.

MAIN SHOPPING STREETS.

The nature of buildings along the main shopping streets has been carefully considered. It is proposed to re-develop the frontages to Lord Street and South Castle Street through the medium of first-class modern shops with offices above them. The area between Lord Street and the Inner Ring Road will provide an ideal setting for worthy office buildings with plenty of light and immediate accessibility, quietness being assured by a grouping of the buildings round a public open space, traversed only by a pedestrian way which will connect Lord Street with the 'bus station and car park.

And here an interesting point arises. It is usual to think of street improvements in terms of *widening*, but one result of taking the heavy traffic off Lord Street and Church Street may well be that it will be found more convenient to the public to *narrow* the carriage-ways, and so to permit for the throngs of shoppers an additional width in the footways.

Although not all these buildings will necessarily be erected at the same time, they will in fact conform to a co-ordinated plan and will, therefore, harmonize in nature, style and heights. This result will be achieved by the Corporation acquiring, under powers now available, all the building sites in the area, and releasing them in suitable parcels subject to conditions designed to secure and maintain such harmony. Far from involving any hardship for lessees, such a scheme will guarantee them security of amenity for all time.

Just inside this area lies the old Bluecoat Hospital which as I indicated is one of Liverpool's oldest, as well as loveliest buildings. Devotees of old Liverpool will be glad to know this is to be carefully restored and

Bird's-eye view of North-eastern portion of redeveloped Central Area

preserved as a memento of the past, its attractiveness enhanced by the creation of a surrounding open space. Instead of being hidden away, as at present, amongst a conglomeration of buildings of no architectural merit, " the Bluecoat " will thus become a detached unit of enhanced dignity from all angles.

A NOBLE CIVIC CENTRE.

No portion of the redevelopment scheme is more striking and distinctive than that of the Civic Centre, based on St. John's Gardens, at the rear of St. George's Hall. The level of the Gardens, together with that of St. John's Lane and William Brown Street is to be lowered. These two streets will cease to be through-traffic ways, and will be entered at each end of St. George's Hall only by flights of steps.

The site of St. John's Gardens will be absorbed into the large open space which fronts and flanks the Mersey Tunnel entrance ; and the whole handsome enclosure will form, on such a scale as Liverpool has never hitherto been able to achieve, the setting for a new, impressive and much-needed ring of civic buildings of co-ordinated design, to supplement the William Brown Street series of classical structures. The new additions will include spacious Municipal Offices to supersede the present building in Dale Street which eventually is to be taken over by the Government. Such is the plan. Like Rome, it will not, of course, materialize in a day but we can visualize it, and prepare accordingly for the day when re-development shall by sheer force of circumstances gather impulse and momentum.

PIER HEAD EXTENSIONS.

That pride of Liverpool, the Pier Head, has for half a century been ripe for some scheme of improvement. It is felt the time has now come for a forward movement worthy of that splendid plateau for hosts of incoming

Bird's-eye view of redeveloped Pier Head

Suggested scheme for the approach to Liverpool Cathedral from Great George Street

voyagers obtaining their first glimpse of Great Britain. An extension of the present dominating trio of buildings is practicable both to north and south, balance of heights and masses being vastly improved thereby. To the north of the Liver Building could be reserved an appropriate site for a new Custom House, to replace the old and inconveniently sited building now being demolished in Canning Place. South of the Mersey Dock Board offices, several blocks of offices could be erected for the shipping and allied interests, at any rate, if part of the site of the Canning Dock were made available.

Among possibilities here should certainly be included a riverside hotel, with restaurants, amid a setting of greenery and flowers. Commanding an unsurpassed river view, it would strike a romantic note which the city could welcome. Supposing we could close the several redundant southern docks, there might also be created, along the riverside, extensive recreational haunts including an open-air swimming pool.

CATHEDRAL APPROACH.

The Liverpool of the future will be exceptional in its possession of two great modern Cathedrals both well outside the inner area. There will be no conflict of architectural styles, and each will have a beauty and grandeur of its own. The erection of the late Sir Edwin Lutyens' Catholic Metropolitan Cathedral on Brownlow Hill is still in an early stage, but Sir Giles Scott's Anglican Cathedral on St. James's Mount is so far advanced that we can already visualize the completed edifice.

For the future layout of the area adjoining the latter, inspiration has been forthcoming. The basis of this layout is a processional approach rising from Great George Street to the Cathedral's main entrance. Commencing with a width sufficient to provide a limited vista of the Cathedral, it rises by several flights of steps to enter a wide square from which the full length of the Cathedral becomes visible. The approach is lined with formal planting while the restful tone of the widened section is emphasized by green lawns, reminiscent of the older Cathedral closes.

This layout is designed to provide a gentle transition from the housing area, west of Great George Street, to the Cathedral itself; and the flight of steps will coincide with the change from residential flats, occupying the lower slopes of the hill, to ecclesiastical buildings, flanking both sides of the upper section of the processional approach. Conforming with the Cathedral motif, the architectural style of these ecclesiastical buildings will be a modern interpretation of Gothic. Those on the left of the approach are intended for a Bishop's Palace and Canons' Residences, while those to the right may conceivably be used for a Choir School and Diocesan Offices. The atmosphere of a Cathedral Close is retained, each group of buildings being sited round a court laid out with peaceful lawns and informal planting.

UNIVERSITY AND HOSPITAL.

Another outstanding section of our re-planning concerns the ever-growing University, also outside the Inner Ring. It is destined for a spectacular as well as an intrinsically great future in conjunction with a projected United Hospital.

Handicapped by its very successes, the University has already long outgrown its own proper buildings; and to-day the vast extension of higher education with which is also interwoven a revolution in medical ideas, calls clamantly for comprehensive developments which must be worthy of the city in whose life these institutions play so vital a part.

As a first step, then, an area of 124 acres is being reserved for the combined requirements of learning and medicine. That area includes the present sites of the University and Royal Infirmary. Bounded on the west by a central area by-pass road, the reserved district contains, for the most part, obsolescent property. It is honeycombed by minor streets all of which will be closed, with the exception of the three main routes ; namely Pembroke Place, West Derby Street, Brownlow Hill, Paddington, Mount Pleasant and Oxford Street.

These three routes, retained as through-traffic ways, will serve to sub-divide the reserved area into four units each approximating thirty acres, and all ripe for re-development after such a pattern of seclusion as will suit both academic and hospital purposes.

ZONING OF INDUSTRIES.

The interests of shipping and allied industries, the life-blood of Merseyside, must obviously be provided for in addition. Ship-building and ship repairing have to be located in the dockside area ; while industries, too, such as grain-milling, sugar-refining and oil-seed-crushing are, for economic reasons, best accommodated near the river. Future policy will therefore, be directed towards widening the dock-side areas in the north to Vauxhall Road, and in the south to Beaufort Street by the gradual extinction of sub-standard houses now encumbering the ground, and the removal of light industries to more inland locations specially planned for their needs and capable of offering a more pleasant life to the workers.

This decanting will permit the expansion of our existing true dock-side industries and enable new-comers also to be accommodated.

Meanwhile, the Liverpool Corporation's quest for new industries, light and varied and supplementary to the basic industries of shipping and transport, has already proved almost sensationally successful. Let us not rest on our laurels, however, we must go on and ever on, if our great population is to be secured against the waste and disheartenment of periodic sectional slackness. The policy of the Corporation has long been, and is, to attract such industries, both new and old, to healthy open surroundings at Speke, Fazakerley, Kirkby and elsewhere on the peri- meter.

Industries displaced in the course of re-developments in the city will be welcomed to these suburban areas. Others at a distance, contemplating migration, may be equally assured of first-class accommodation, cordial encouragement and the best of conditions. Capitalists and operatives already there are alike loud in their praise of Liverpool's trading estates. Speke is rapidly filling up, and Kirkby, though as yet but a nucleus, has already its own internal 'bus service, and is assured of a brilliant future.

RESIDENTIAL COLONIES.

It remains for me, in this brief forecast of the future only to add a few words about prospective living-conditions in our new city. Of necessity, the people will have their homes, churches, schools, halls, cinemas, shops, playgrounds and so forth within the areas enclosed by the Radial and Ring Roads about which I have been writing, and which can be visualized as so many ribs of a fan. In the inner areas, ancient slums and obsolescent property abound. Further out is a belt of buildings, extending approximately to Queen's Drive, which, though erected under more stringent regulations, will become obsolete during the next few decades.

Model of Speke showing Stadium on the river front

Speke—a suggestion for the Parish Church

from a drawing by J. L. Berbiers

We may, therefore, anticipate re-development, during the coming fifty years, of the whole area within the Queen's Drive ring. The congested small cottage properties in the inner spaces will give place to blocks of flats, set in garden surroundings, and widely spaced to secure ample air and sunshine. And, of course, there will be playing fields, and school buildings of a light and airy order, standing in their own grounds. For displaced families, provision must and can be made in rural areas at present beyond the civic pale. The improved system of arterial and belt roads will vouchsafe the necessary mobility.

SOWING THE SEEDS.

How far these partially enclosed spaces will become self-contained communities, with interests, characters and outlooks of their own, the future alone can determine. I feel, however, satisfied that they will be infinitely cleaner, healthier, happier and more sheltered places of residence than those of to-day.   It will not be surprising if the people, instead of feeling lost in a very Sahara of bricks and mortar, should automatically form themselves into neighbourhood units, or self-conscious wards, animated by a new and perhaps competitive civic pride, and together forming a federal city a sort of microcosm of the British Empire itself.

This framework or skeleton, given the necessary finance, can be created by local administration, but the *modus vivendi*, the task of maintaining and lubricating the economic machinery essential to the lives of the people rests with the higher statesmanship.   If our standard of living is to be maintained, and national solvency safeguarded, we must have knowledge and wisdom at the helm ; and the only sure way of securing that is, not only to provide worthy environments for our citizens, but to educate and train the enfranchised masses in political sanity, and in ways of industriousness, self-reliance, self-respect and good citizenship generally. Towards this long-term task, the Liverpool of to-day is preparing to do its share, content to sow the seeds so that the Liverpool and Britain of to-morrow may enjoy a bumper harvest.

In the words of our own Lancashire poets :—

I can see the city of my dream arising
'Neath these smoky northern skies,
And my heart is all aglow with strange surmising
Of its golden destinies,
I have heard the crash of ancient buildings falling,
And, above the dust and roar,
I can hear the city's voice in music calling
To the years that lie before.

And the least of us, my friends, may help to build it,
And the nation yet shall see
How its sons, with one consent, arose and willed it,
And the city came to be !

And the gates of it shall not be shut at all by day . for
there shall be no night there
And they shall bring the glory and honour of the nations
into it.

REVELATION, Chapter 21

CENTRAL LIVERPOOL
— FUTURE PLAN —

RIVER MERSEY

EXCHANGE RAILWAY STATION

TITHEBARN

CHAPEL ST

DALE STREET

WATER ST

PIER HEAD

GOREE

JAMES ST

LORD ST

WH

STRAND ST

PARADISE ST

N